1. Welcome to stamp collecting

Collecting stamps is a very enjoyable hobby for people of all ages. Building a collection is a creative way of spending your time and it will give you a lot of satisfaction.

It's one of the most interesting ways to learn about other countries – their people, their scenery, their wildlife. World history shows itself on the album page, with pictures of famous men and events of the recent past and back through ancient times. Many stamps are exciting works of art on a small scale. Most sports have been shown on stamps, Olympic issues being especially popular. Beautiful pictures of animals, birds and butterflies appear on others.

Famous people on stamps. Sir Winston Churchill (Great Britain, 1974) and Michael Jackson (St. Vincent, 1985).

There are three basic ways of stamp collecting – (1) a general collection – collecting stamps of all countries and periods, in other words saving all stamps that come your way; (2) country collecting – collecting the stamps of one or a few countries, : stamps of a particular peric – collecting stamps of all design subject – for exam flowers etc. Most peopl collection. This is the appr this booklet.

But first a few words about how stamps came about and the different types of stamps.

2. The first stamps

People have written letters for thousands of years – before paper was invented messages were inscribed on clay tablets and during the Middle Ages on parchment. The medieval kings employed messengers to take instructions from London to important people in the provinces and gradually the Royal messenger service evolved into a service for the general public. King Charles I in 1635 "opened" his Royal Post to all who could afford to use it and his son Charles II set up the General Letter Office which is now the Royal Mail we know today.

However, it was not until 1840 that stamps were introduced – the famous Penny Black and Twopenny

Blue, both of which featured a portrait of Queen Victoria. At the time the Post Office called them "labels" rather than stamps and the gum on the back was known as "cement".

Soon other countries started to issue stamps – Brazil followed in 1843, Belgium and France in 1849. The first Brazilian stamps were of a curious design which has earned them the nickname "Bullseyes". The first Belgian stamps showed the King and the first French issue Cerès. The first British Colony to issue stamps was the island of Mauritius in 1847 – its first stamps, modelled on the Penny Black, are famous rarities.

Since 1840 well over ¼ million different postage stamps have been issued by some 600 countries. Some

A 1d. Black and a 2d. Blue, the world's first postage stamps.

countries have been amalgamated into others and so have ceased to issue stamps (known to collectors as "dead countries"). Today there are some 200 "active" stamp issuing territories from Afghanistan to Zimbabwe. Try making a list from your existing knowledge – then check it against the list at the back of this book.

No sooner was the Penny Black issued than a few people started to collect stamps but it was not until the 1860s that the hobby became popular – at first in France

where collectors were called timbrologists (*timbre* is the french for stamps). Soon the craze spread to Britain and gradually around the world. No one knows exactly how many collectors there are but stamp collecting is still reckoned to be the most popular collecting hobby.

3. Different types of stamps

Basically stamps are of three types: **definitives** – the everyday stamps; **commemoratives** – larger sized stamps issued to mark a particular anniversary or event and **specials** – again larger size, issued to depict the life of a country, its animals, buildings, scenery, etc. This last

Special

Definitive

Commemorative

2

type are of particular interest to thematic collectors and are sometimes referred to as "thematic stamps".

Examples of commemorative and special stamps relating to two themes – famous people and wildlife – are shown below.

Famous people on stamps: Albert Einstein, scientist (Italy, 1979), Robert Louis Stevenson, writer (Samoa, 1969), Charles Darwin, scientist (Ascension, 1982) and Sir Walter Raleigh, explorer (G.B., 1973).

Wildlife on stamps: Birds – Kingfisher (G.B., 1980); Fish – Yellow Banded Goatfish (Fiji, 1985); Insects – Leather Beetle (Sweden, 1987) and Mammals – Brown Hare (G.B., 1979).

4. Getting started

The best way to start your collection is with a large packet of stamps which you can buy at stamp shops and from good toy and hobby shops. Always buy the largest you can afford – to ensure you have the maximum number of stamps to start your collection. You will have great fun sorting them out into countries. Many collectors begin with a "starter pack" which in addition to a packet of stamps also contains an album, tweezers and hinges. We will say more about albums and hinges later. Firstly here is a brief word about tweezers. Take the stamps out of the packet and get used to handling them with the tweezers; you will soon find it easier to pick up single stamps in this way than using your fingers. The other reason for using tweezers is that everybody's fingers have some moisture and grease on them which could spoil stamps picked up by hand. Even using tweezers, of course, your hands should be clean before you start sorting your stamps.

Now let's start to look at the stamps. You will see that most of them have parts of postmarks on them. The Post Office puts postmarks on stamps to show where and when the letter was posted, but also to stop people using them again.

Stamps that have been postmarked are called "used" stamps. Some people call the postmark a "cancellation", so they say the stamps are "cancelled".

You may find in your packet some stamps which have not been "used" or "cancelled"; a stamp collector calls these stamps "mint" or "unused". Look for examples in the stamps you have.

Left, a used stamp with a neat postmark.
Right, an unused stamp.

The condition of a stamp is very important and a good collector will put to one side stamps which are torn, creased or have corners missing.

If you get a stamp in poor condition do not mount it in your album but do not throw it away. Keep it aside until you can find a better example.

Used stamps with neat postmarks are much more attractive than those with messy ones. Some postmarks, especially on parcels, are heavy and inky so that a beautiful stamp is very easily spoiled. If any of your used stamps has such a postmark try to get a better example for your collection.

Mint or used, you should always make sure your stamp still has the clear, fresh colours in which it was

Left, stamp with clear postmark, worthy of collecting. Right, stamp with poor postmark – save only until you have a better one.

printed. Stamps kept in bright sunlight (like shop windows) usually fade and look dull and flat. Stamps can also easily become stained and discoloured. This often happens if they are kept in a leather wallet without protection. Always keep your stamps in an album or stockbook or in clean envelopes.

So, sharpen your skill at observation. Always aim for stamps in good condition!

5. Finding more stamps

Although your stamp packet gave you a good start you will want to add more stamps to your collection.

In your local post office watch for posters and leaflets advertising forthcoming special issues. In Britain, the Royal Mail issues about eight sets a year. If you can afford them and want to collect them, buy them as soon as they appear. Some special issues are very popular and quickly sell out.

Let your family, relations and friends know that you are now a keen stamp collector. Ask them to keep any stamps they receive on their mail for you, especially if the letters are from abroad. Don't worry if stamps offered to you are ones you already have as having several of the same stamp means you can choose the best one to mount in your album.

It also gives you stamps to swap with other collectors. There are no hard and fast rules about swapping, only that the exchange is a fair one. For very common stamps the normal rule is one for one. You give one and you get one.

But remember what was said earlier about "condition". It would be unfair to offer a torn or heavily postmarked stamp, and expect to get a perfect example of something else in exchange. Where stamps are more valuable the prices in a stamp catalogue will guide you in making a fair swap.

Finally, you might buy stamps from a local stamp dealer or by post from one who advertises in a stamp magazine. You will inevitably have to obtain from dealers specific stamps that you want for your collection.

Some dealers will send you "approvals" – books containing stamps which are priced individually. This is a good way of adding some better stamps to your collection. However, if it is quantity rather than quality that appeals to you, ask your dealer for "Kiloware" –

large envelopes/bags containing stamps on paper – you may well find some interesting items although be prepared for much duplication. "Kiloware" differs from "stamp packets" in that stamps from packets are normally "off paper".

6. Preparing your stamps

People often give you stamps torn off envelopes. Before you mount them in your album you need to remove them from the envelope paper. Never try to pull the stamps off, you will damage them. Always float them off.

Pour some clean water (warm but *not* hot) into a bowl, then float each stamp (face uppermost) on the surface of the water. You can float as many stamps at one time as you have room for.

Leave the stamps for fifteen minutes or so to give the water time to soak the gum that is sticking the stamp to the paper. Most stamps can then be gently peeled away. If they do not come away easily do not try to tear them off the paper. Leave them for another five minutes or so and try again.

Providing your hands are clean it's better to handle the stamps with your fingers when peeling off the envelope paper. The paper of stamps is weakened when it is damp and picking them up with your tweezers may damage them.

When you have peeled the stamps off the envelope there will probably be some damp gum still on the back of them. Let the stamp float on the water for a few minutes – the gum will dissolve away. However, do not immerse the stamp in water. For most stamps this would be safe enough but for some it would be dangerous as the ink may run.

Then shake off any excess water and place the stamps face upwards on a sheet of clean blotting paper or kitchen paper towel. This is why it is so important to clean all the gum off. If you do not, your stamps will stick to the blotting paper and you will have to float them off all over again. When all the stamps are laid out cover them with more clean blotting paper or kitchen paper towel and place a heavy book on top. This will flatten the stamps as they dry. After half an hour carefully remove the stamps with tweezers. Spread them out on another piece of clean, dry blotting paper and leave to dry in the air for a little while. When completely dry they are ready for mounting in your album.

Floating off stamps.

There are two things which you must be very careful about when floating stamps. Firstly, many old stamps were printed in special inks which run, change colour, or even disappear completely in water. Fewer modern stamps are affected in this way but even so it is best to be safe, so avoid letting water get on the surface of the stamp when you are floating-off. Secondly, be careful when floating stamps to keep separate stamps affixed to white and coloured envelopes. Take out any stamps which are stuck to bits of coloured paper and float these separately. Be suspicious of any highly coloured paper, like those blue "airmail" labels. Floating can easily make the ink run and so damage your stamps by staining them with unwanted colours.

Finally, always think twice before tearing a stamp off an envelope. Most old stamps and some modern ones too, if they have interesting postmarks, will be more valuable if left on the envelope. If in doubt always try to ask a more experienced collector's advice.

Having acquired and prepared your stamps the next stage is sorting them.

7. Sorting stamps

You are now ready to sort your stamps. This means separating them into the countries which issued them.

Make a clear space on the table because you need to spread the stamps out. See if you can find twenty or thirty envelopes for storage, too. If you start with new ones you can use them over and over again during your collecting. But old (used) envelopes are just as good. If the envelopes are all about the same size keep them tidy in a box. A shoe box is useful for this, as well as for keeping stamps before sorting.

Stamps of Great Britain are identified by the head of the monarch. From left to right: (top row) Queen Victoria, King Edward VII, King George V, King Edward VIII (bottom row) King George VI, Queen Elizabeth II.

Spread the stamps on the table in front of you, using tweezers. You may know a few of them at once because they are from your own country. Write its name on one of the envelopes and put the stamps in it.

Now look and see how many other countries you can recognise. Lots of stamps have the country name printed on them in English. Every time you recognise a country write its name on one of the envelopes and put all its stamps in it. Remember British stamps do not have the country name but always have the head of the Queen (or King).

If the wording is in a foreign language you don't know, you may need help at first. Here are a few examples:

België/Belgique	Belgium
Ceskoslovensko	Czechoslovakia
Danmark	Denmark
DDR	East Germany
Deutsche Bundespost	West Germany
España	Spain
Foroyar	Faröe Islands
Magyar Posta	Hungary
Nederland	Netherlands
Norge or Noreg	Norway
Polska	Poland
Posta Romana or RP Romina ..	Rumania
Poste Italiane	Italy
Republik Indonesia	Indonesia
Republik Österreich	Austria
République Française or RF ...	France

Albania

Japan

North Korea

Greece

All these are easy to learn but some stamps will be from countries whose alphabets you do not know. Some very common ones with unfamiliar alphabets are illustrated to help you.

Stanley Gibbons publish a little book called *Stamp Collecting – How to Identify Stamps* which will be useful while you are still learning.

Some guidance on identifying stamps may be included in your stamp album so be sure to look there.

Sometimes the currency will give you a clue to the country. Details of the currencies are to be found in the Stamp Countries list at the back of this book.

Russia

China (People's Republic)

Stamps from Albania, Japan, North Korea, Greece, Russia, and China (People's Republic).

8. Mounting stamps

When the stamps have been sorted they are ready for mounting in their proper places in the album. As a new collector you have probably bought a "printed album" with pages that have the country names printed on them.

Take one envelope at a time and turn to the page of the album where the country is shown. Say you have five stamps, you can mount them neatly side by side on that page. There are lines already printed there to help in placing them upright. Do not crowd them too close together; leave a space of one or two of the little squares between the stamps on the row and between rows to help the page look neat.

Very often stamps are issued in "sets". For example, Great Britain issued a "set" in 1989 showing birds. There were four stamps with "face values" of 19p, 27p, 32p and 35p.

If you have them all you have a "complete set". Mount them next to one another and put them in order, 19p first, then 27p, then 32p, then 35p. Collectors mostly mount sets this way.

Always use good quality stamp hinges to mount your stamps, never use glue, sticky tape, stamp edging or the gum of the stamps themselves because if you want to move them you will damage both the stamp and the album page.

To mount a stamp using a stamp hinge, first turn it face downwards. Take a hinge and fold over a flap of

A "complete set".

about a quarter of an inch with the gummed side outwards. Moisten the flap slightly with the tip of the tongue, but only along the lower edge. Do not make it too wet because moisture might spill over on to the gum of a mint stamp and cause it to stick to the album page. Fix the moistened flap close to the top edge of the back of the stamp. Place it centrally near this edge but keep it clear of the perforations.

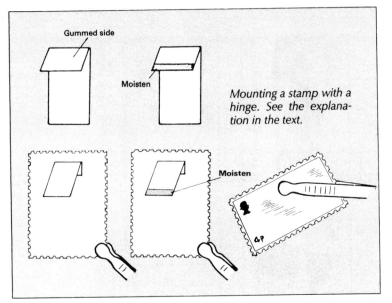

Gummed side

Moisten

Mounting a stamp with a hinge. See the explanation in the text.

Moisten

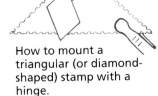

How to mount a triangular (or diamond-shaped) stamp with a hinge.

Now unfold the hinge and turn the stamp over with the tweezers. The gummed side of the hinge is now facing you. Pick the stamp up (again with the tweezers) and lightly moisten the free end of the hinge with your tongue. Fold the hinge down again and, keeping it flat against the back of the stamp by holding both in the tweezers, position the stamp at its place on the page and press the front of it just enough for the hinge to grip. Then turn the stamp up with the tweezers and use your fingers to press the hinge firmly on to the page to make it stick properly. Never try to remove a hinge from a stamp or album page while it is still wet as this will damage them. Leave it for an hour to dry first and it will peel off easily.

When you turn the stamp down again you see why collectors use hinges for mounting. The stamp is kept firmly in place but can easily be turned up to see the back. By moistening the hinge at the two edges mentioned this turning back will do no damage to the perforations.

Be careful about placing the hinges when mounting diamond-shaped or triangular stamps. So as to avoid creasing when you turn them back, put the hinges along one side, not at the point.

Good quality hinges will not damage unused stamps when removed – but they will leave a slight mark. Nowadays, many collectors prefer "unmounted mint" stamps and so never use stamp hinges but specially produced transparent stamp mounts, such as "Lighthouse" mounts. You are advised to use these to protect the more valuable unused stamps in your collection.

9. Stamp albums

As we have mentioned most new collectors begin with a printed album which will be satisfactory for a while. However, as your collection grows it will become difficult to find space for all your stamps, especially those of popular countries such as G.B., France, Germany, India, Poland, the U.S.A., etc. The next stage is a loose-leaf printed album – this will enable you to add more pages and to split your collection into two or more album binders if necessary.

More advanced collectors like albums with plain pages which they can "write up" themselves – the name of the country, the year of issue of the stamps, etc. When the time comes for you to develop your collection in this way seek advice from other collectors, your local stamp dealer and by looking at the advertisements in stamp magazines. Always try to examine any new albums before you buy them to make sure they are suitable for you.

10. The stamp catalogue

Collectors looking for information about their stamps turn to catalogues. Stanley Gibbons have been publishing these for over 125 years.

See if your school or public library has the one called Stanley Gibbons *Simplified Catalogue – Stamps of the World*. This is the best one for new collectors. It is a big book published every year in three volumes (Vol. 1 Foreign Countries A–J; Vol. 2 Foreign Countries K–Z and Vol. 3 Commonwealth Countries). Stamps right back to the 1840 "Penny Black" are illustrated and listed for you and it is quite easy to understand.

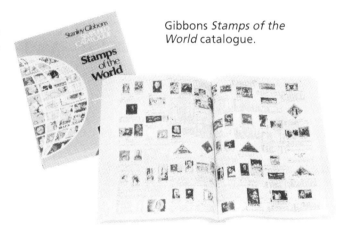

Gibbons *Stamps of the World* catalogue.

All the countries are set out in alphabetical order, and the stamps of each country are then listed in the order in which they were issued. The earliest dates are therefore first, continuing through the years right down to the present time. This catalogue lists the stamps of both "active" and "dead" countries – some 600 countries in all.

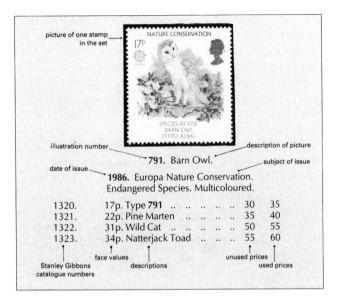

An extract from *Stamps of the World*, showing the listing of a complete set and what the different entries mean.

Read the notes printed at the beginning of the catalogue very carefully. They explain what the lists mean and how they are set out. When you are trying to find a stamp in the catalogue the illustrations are the main guide. But do look closely at your stamp first. See if it has a date printed somewhere in the design, as this may tell you which year to look up straight away. British stamps have included the year in the design since 1987.

Stamps of the World is specially simplified to make it helpful to beginners. Stanley Gibbons also publish many other detailed catalogues and you will want to use these as you become more advanced.

What should you do if you cannot find a stamp in *Stamps of the World*? Firstly, check very thoroughly. It is such a large book that you might just have overlooked your stamp. Make sure you are looking in the right country, for example, there's an index of countries to help you. It is possible that the stamp was issued after your catalogue was printed, particularly if you are using an old one. Always use the most up-to-date catalogue possible.

Gibbons do not stock the stamps of certain countries which they feel issue far too many for their postal use. These stamps are not listed in the main part of the catalogue but in an Appendix list at the end of the listing for that country. It may be worth looking to see if your stamp is listed there.

Possibly your stamp is not really a postage stamp at all. It has to be a postage stamp to be in the Gibbons Catalogue. As you know, a postage stamp is one that will pay for carrying mail through the post. Your stamp might be a charity or advertising label or a "revenue", "local" or "bogus" stamp.

A "revenue" stamp, such as a savings or insurance stamp, has nothing to do with the post. Lots of countries use stamps to pay fees on various legal documents. Look for words like "revenue", "fee" or "documentary". Many countries, however, use the same stamps for revenue purposes as they do for postage and sometimes include the words "revenue" in the design. As long as the stamp contains the word "postage" as well you should be able to find it in the catalogue.

A "local" stamp is one which only pays postage in a limited area and is not recognised elsewhere. Proper postage stamps, as listed in the catalogue, pay for carrying mail anywhere in the world.

A "bogus" stamp is designed to look like a postage stamp but is printed only for sale to collectors and not authorised or sold by the Post Office. Many, in fact, come from countries which do not even exist. Learn as much as you can about these so you are not taken in by them.

All these items are what is known as "cinderella stamps" – popular with some collectors but beginners should not concern themselves too much with them. There is enough to learn about postage stamps. In time, however, you might find that the "cinderellas" have great interest.

11. Stamp prices

In the Stanley Gibbons catalogues such as *Stamps of the World* you will see that stamps are given prices. The prices on the left are for unused stamps and those on the right are for the same stamps in used condition.

These prices are the ones at which Stanley Gibbons sell the stamps when they are in stock. They are carefully checked before each new edition of a catalogue is published and altered if necessary. So you need to look at the latest edition of a catalogue if you want to know the current price of stamps.

The price at which Gibbons will sell a stamp (the catalogue price) is based on what it will cost them to replace that stamp in their stock and since Gibbons are buying stamps all the time from post offices, from collectors, from other stamp dealers and through auctions they are in a very good position to judge what the selling price of a particular stamp should be.

Remember that the catalogue prices refer to stamps in good condition; stamps in poor condition are worth much less!

People who have never studied the subject often think it is easy to make a fortune from stamps. They tell you that because a stamp is old it must be valuable. Don't believe them! Check in the catalogue first and remember what you learnt about "condition" earlier. The older the stamp, the more likely it is in poor condition and not worth much.

A mistake in printing a stamp can often make it more valuable. In 1963, for instance, there was a British 3d. stamp issued in honour of the Red Cross Centenary. It should have had a large red cross in the design but some were issued by mistake without it. This is an "error" and because there are so few of them a collector would have to pay a lot of money if he wanted one for his collection.

Less spectacular than errors but also very interesting are "varieties"; these are stamps which, due to a fault in their production, differ in detail from the normal. The

The Great Britain 1963 Red Cross 3d. stamp. Left, normal. Right, error with cross omitted.

Variety – Second stamp of second row has value 1.78 ft instead of 1.70 ft as other stamps (Hungary, 1953).

differences can be quite small but if you know what to look for you can spot things which other people do not notice.

Varieties are not worth as much as errors but are of greater value than normal stamps. Details of new varieties discovered are published each month in *Gibbons Stamp Monthly*.

One question often asked is "are used or unused stamps worth more?"

There's no easy answer. It depends on the country. When you have a big country like the U.S.A., millions of stamps are used on letters every day. So used stamps are very common and liable to be cheaper to buy than the unused ones. But a tiny island like Tristan da Cunha doesn't use many stamps in a year, so these are harder to buy than their unused stamps. Age may be important, too. With very old stamps – say of the last century – few unused examples may now survive. Because of this collectors will pay a lot more for them than they would for used examples.

12. Covers and postmarks

Some collectors like to collect stamps still affixed to envelopes – normally referred to as "covers". There are several reasons for this but as a general rule it would be wise to keep old stamps on cover until you can be sure that they are not worth any more on cover than they would be soaked off.

Victorian 1d., red-brown on cover – not to be soaked off!

The most interesting thing about covers is usually the postmark. As well as the normal "operational" postmarks in daily use, many post offices also use "special" postmarks – for example on the day of issue of new stamps or at stamp and other exhibitions. A cover bearing new stamps used on the first day is known as a "first day cover". Most main post offices sell special first day cover envelopes to which you can affix the stamps and post them on the first day to receive a special postmark. Special first day posting boxes are provided at most main post offices.

There is not room here to go into details about postmarks but a few examples of "operational" and "special" postmarks are shown.

If you do not save the entire cover bearing an

British First Day Cover.

Foreign handstamp.

G.B. handstamp.

G.B. machine.

Foreign special.

Foreign machine.

G.B. special.

interesting postmark you should cut a neat rectangle round the stamp/postmark as shown here. Never cut to a fancy shape around the postmark.

Most countries sell cards and envelopes with stamps already printed on them — these are known as "postal stationery" and are best collected complete. If the stamp is cut off, the same rules apply as to postmarks — cut in rectangular shape.

13. Useful philatelic terms

Here are some of the words you will come across in stamp books, catalogues and magazines. For a more detailed list, see the Stanley Gibbons book *Stamp Collecting – Philatelic Terms Illustrated.*

ADHESIVE. A stamp intended to be affixed by means of gum, as distinct from one printed or embossed on postal stationery.

AIRMAIL STAMP. A stamp intended for use on letters or parcels to be carried by air.

APPROVALS. The name given to selections of stamps sent by a dealer to a collector. The collector pays for those he wishes to keep and returns the remainder within a pre-arranged time limit.

BILINGUAL. A stamp inscribed (with the country name, currency, etc.) in two languages.

BISECT. A stamp cut in half and usually used for half its face value.

BOGUS. Labels purporting to be postage stamps but which are not. Also known as "phantom stamps".

BOOKLET. Stamps are sold by many countries for convenience in booklets.

They are often sold from slot machines outside post offices.

BOOKLET PANE. Two or more stamps joined together (and sometimes joined to advertising labels), which make up a "page" in a stamp booklet.

CACHET. A device, often pictorial, handstamped on an envelope or card indicating that it has been carried in special circumstances.

A booklet pane (G.B.).

CANCELLATION. A defacing mark on a stamp to prevent its re-use.

CHARITY STAMP. A stamp sold for more than its postal value, with the difference going to charity.

CINDERELLA STAMPS. All categories of stamps and labels which are not listed by general stamp catalogues, particularly those of Stanley Gibbons. These include local, telegraph and railway stamps, fiscals, forgeries and bogus items, essays and proofs, labels and seals, etc.

COMMEMORATIVE STAMP. A stamp which marks a special event or anniversary.

Charity stamp (Finland).

17

COVER. The stamp collector's name for an envelope used in the post.

DEFINITIVE STAMP. An "everyday" stamp, usually small and functional, as opposed to a commemorative or charity stamp.

DIE. The engraved original from which printing plates are produced.

EMBOSSING. Stamping a design in coloured or colourless relief.

ERROR. A mistake on a stamp, either by the designer or by the printer.

ESSAY. A suggested design for a stamp.

EXCHANGE PACKET. A packet, usually circulating amongst the members of a philatelic society, in which members offer duplicates or unwanted items for sale to other members.

FACE VALUE. The postal value printed on a stamp.

FAKE. A genuine stamp which has been altered in some way, or has had something added to it (for example a faked cancellation). This is usually done fraudulently to increase its value.

FISCAL STAMPS. Stamps used for non-postal purposes, such as payment of court fees, licence fees,

Definitive stamps – U.S.A. and Sweden.

British greetings stamp (Cupid).

etc. Also known as *revenue stamps*. Some postage stamps are equally valid for postal and fiscal use.

FORGERY. A fraudulent imitation of a stamp design, made to defraud the postal authorities or collectors.

GRAPHITE LINES. Vertical black lines printed on the backs of some British stamps, 1957–61, to activate sorting machinery.

GREETINGS STAMP. Stamp specially designed for use on greetings mail, such as birthday, get well or congratulations cards.

IMPRINT. Inscription of the printer's name on the sheet margin or in the margin of each stamp.

INSCRIPTION. Any words or figures printed on a stamp.

KILOWARE. Bundles of stamps "on paper", sold by weight.

LOCAL STAMPS. Stamps whose validity is restricted to a particular area and which are not valid for general national or international mail.

MACHINS. Series name given to the British definitive issues begun in 1967, which bear a portrait of the Queen designed from a plaster-cast by Arnold Machin. See *Wildings* below.

MINIATURE SHEET. A small sheet containing very few stamps, perhaps only one, usually with decorative borders. Sometimes erroneously known as a *souvenir sheet*. Miniature sheets are sold intact at post office counters. *Souvenir Sheets* are similar in appearance to miniature sheets but are not usually issued by a post office and have no postal validity.

NON-VALUE INDICATOR STAMP. A stamp not having a specific face value but a coding to indicate the postage paid – for example 'A' or '1ST'.

OBSOLETE. No longer in current use.

OVERPRINT. Something, other than the face value, printed on a stamp subsequent to manufacture. See also *Surcharge* (see overleaf).

British "2nd" (second class) NVI stamp.

PANE. Part of a sheet of stamps, surrounded by a margin. Also used to denote a block of stamps from a booklet.

PERFIN. Stamp punctured with initials or a design by means of tiny holes. The punctures are applied by private or public concerns to discourage fraudulent use of such stamps by employees.

PHOSPHOR. A chemical applied as *bands*, later as *all-over phosphor* (band covering the entire stamp) to

Perfin – JPII, private perforation to commemorate visit of Pope John Paul II, 1982.

printed stamps. More recently introduced is *phosphorised paper*, with phosphor added to the paper coating before the stamps are printed. The bands can normally be seen when the stamp is held at an angle to the light. Phosphor is used in automatic sorting of mail at "mechanised" post offices.

PHQ CARDS. Picture cards, usable as postcards, showing enlarged colour reproductions of newly issued British stamps. PHQ means "Postal Headquarters", used with identifying serial numbers.

POSTAGE DUES. Stamps affixed by postal officials to indicate that unpaid postage or a fine is due for payment on delivery.

POSTAL FISCALS. Fiscal stamps used for postal purposes.

POSTAL FORGERY. A forgery used or intended to be used to defraud the postal authorities.

POSTAL HISTORY. A strange term, normally used to describe covers sent before the introduction of stamps or stamped covers bearing interesting postal markings.

POSTAL STATIONERY. Postal envelopes, cards, wrappers, etc., having impressed or imprinted stamps on them.

Imprinted 15(c) stamp on U.S. postcard.

POSTMARK. Any mark struck upon letters, etc., passing through the post. Normally used to cancel postage stamps.

PRE-CANCELLED. Obliterated by the Post Office

19

before issue, used by firms posting matter in bulk.

PROOFS. Trial impressions taken at various stages during the manufacture of a stamp.

PROVISIONALS. Temporary emergency stamps, often created by overprinting or surcharging existing stamps.

SELF-ADHESIVE. A stamp issued on backing paper from which it can be peeled off and reaffixed to mail.

SE-TENANT. Stamps of different denominations, or showing different varieties, joined together in a pair or a larger multiple.

SPACEFILLER. A substandard copy of a stamp intended as a "stop-gap" until a better one is found, or as a substitute for an otherwise costly item. Also, the very commonest of stamps, the abundant supply of which will rapidly fill spaces in the album.

Se-tenant pair (Mauritania postage due stamps).

SPECIMEN. Sample stamp bearing the word "specimen", or the equivalent in another language.

SURCHARGE. An overprint which alters or confirms the face value of a stamp.

TELEGRAPH STAMPS. Used for the pre-payment of telegraph fees.

TÊTE-BÊCHE. Stamps joined together but printed upside-down in relation to one another.

THEMATIC COLLECTING. Collecting stamps having a particular design theme (e.g. birds) rather than collecting by country of issue. Known as "topical collecting" in the U.S.A.

USED ABROAD. Stamps of one country used in another, usually identified by the postmark.

VARIETY. Any stamp showing differences from the normal.

VIGNETTE. The central portion of a stamp, usually of a bi-coloured stamp (the outer portion is known as the *frame*).

WILDINGS. Series name given to British definitives (1952–67), bearing a portrait of the Queen by photographer Dorothy Wilding. Succeeded by *Machin* stamps (see above).

Wilding stamp.

Machin stamp.

14. Stamp countries and currencies

This list shows the countries of the world which are issuing stamps today and gives the currencies which they use. These are often a useful aid in identifying the country, although you will find that many countries shorten or leave out the currency name and show "10 cents", for example, as "10c." or just "10".

Afghanistan	100 puls = 1 afghani
Aitutaki	100 cents = 1 New Zealand dollar
Aland	100 penni = 1 markka
Albania	100 qind = 1 lek
Alderney	100 pence = 1 pound sterling
Algeria	100 centimes = 1 dinar
Andorra	French and Spanish currency used
Angola	100 luei = 1 kwanza
Anguilla	100 cents = 1 East Caribbean dollar
Antigua	100 cents = 1 East Caribbean dollar
Argentina	100 centavos = 1 austral
Aruba	Netherlands currency used
Ascension	100 pence = 1 pound sterling
Australia	100 cents = 1 Australian dollar
Australian Antarctic Territory	Australian currency used
Austria	100 groschen = 1 schilling
Azores	100 centavos = 1 escudo
Bahamas	100 cents = 1 Bahamas dollar
Bahrain	1000 fils = 1 dinar
Bangladesh	100 paisa = 1 taka
Barbados	100 cents = 1 Barbados dollar
Barbuda	100 cents = 1 East Caribbean dollar
Belgium	100 centimes = 1 franc

Belize	100 cents = 1 Belize dollar
Bénin	100 centimes = 1 CFA franc
Bermuda	100 cents = 1 Bermudan dollar
Bhutan	100 chetrum = 1 ngultrum
Bolivia	100 centavos = 1 peso
Bophuthatswana	100 cents = 1 South African rand
Botswana	100 thebe = 1 pula
Brazil	100 centavos = 1 cruzado
British Antarctic Territory	British currency used
British Virgin Islands	100 cents = 1 U.S. dollar
Brunei	100 cents = 1 Brunei dollar
Bulgaria	100 stotinki = 1 lev
Burkina Faso	100 centimes = 1 CFA franc
Burma	100 pyas = 1 kyat
Burundi	100 centimes = 1 Burundi franc
Cameroun	100 centimes = 1 CFA franc
Canada	100 cents = 1 Canadian dollar
Cape Verde Islands	100 centavos = 1 escudo
Cayman Islands	100 cents = 1 Cayman Islands dollar
Central African Republic	100 centimes = 1 CFA franc
Chad	100 centimes = 1 CFA franc
Chile	100 centavos = 1 peso
China (People's Republic)	100 fen = 1 yuan
China (Taiwan)	100 cents = 1 yuan
Christmas Island	Australian currency used
Ciskei	100 cents = 1 South African rand
Cocos (Keeling) Islands	Australian currency used
Colombia	100 centavos = 1 peso
Comoro Islands	100 centimes = 1 CFA franc
Congo Republic	100 centimes = 1 CFA franc
Cook Islands	100 cents = 1 New Zealand dollar
Costa Rica	100 centimos = 1 colón
Cuba	100 centavos = 1 peso
Cyprus	1000 mils = 1 Cypriot pound
Czechoslovakia	100 haleru = 1 koruna
Denmark	100 öre = 1 krone
Djibouti	100 centimes = 1 Djibouti franc
Dominica	100 cents = 1 East Caribbean dollar
Dominican Republic	100 centavos = 1 peso

Ecuador	100 centavos = 1 sucre
Egypt	100 piastres = 1 Egyptian pound
El Salvador	100 centavos = 1 colon
Equatorial Guinea	100 centimes = 1 CFA franc
Ethiopia	100 cents = 1 birr
Falkland Islands	100 pence = 1 pound sterling
Faröe Islands	Danish currency used
Fiji	100 cents = 1 Fijian dollar
Finland	100 penni = 1 markka
France	100 centimes = 1 franc
French Polynesia	100 centimes = 1 CFP franc
French Southern and Antarctic Territories	French currency used
Gabon	100 centimes = 1 CFA franc
Gambia	100 bututs = 1 dalasi
Germany (East)	100 pfennig = 1 Ostmark
Germany (West)	100 pfennig = 1 Deutschmark
Ghana	100 pesewas = 1 cedi
Gibraltar	100 pence = 1 pound sterling
Great Britain	100 pence = 1 pound sterling
Greece	100 lepta = 1 drachma
Greenland	Danish currency used
Grenada	100 cents = 1 East Caribbean dollar
Grenada Grenadines	100 cents = 1 East Caribbean dollar
Guatemala	100 centavos = 1 quetzal
Guernsey	100 pence = 1 pound sterling
Guinea	100 centimes = 1 franc
Guinea-Bissau	100 cents = 1 peso
Guyana	100 cents = 1 Guyanese dollar
Haiti	100 centimes = 1 gourde
Honduras	100 centavos = 1 lempira
Hong Kong	100 cents = 1 Hong Kong dollar
Hungary	100 filler = 1 forint
Iceland	100 aurar = 1 krona
India	100 paisa = 1 rupee
Indonesia	100 sen = 1 rupiah
Iran	100 dinars = 1 rial

Iraq	1000 fils = 1 dinar
Ireland	100 pence = 1 Irish pound (punt)
Isle of Man	100 pence = 1 pound sterling
Israel	100 agora = 1 shekel
Italy	100 centesimi = 1 lira
Ivory Coast	100 centimes = 1 CFA franc
Jamaica	100 cents = 1 Jamaican dollar
Japan	100 sen = 1 yen
Jersey	100 pence = 1 pound sterling
Jordan	1000 fils = 1 dinar
Kampuchea	100 cents = 1 riel
Kenya	100 cents = 1 Kenya shilling
Kiribati	100 cents = 1 Australian dollar
Korea (North)	100 chon = 1 North Korean won
Korea (South)	100 chon = 1 South Korean won
Kuwait	1000 fils = 1 dinar
Laos	100 cents = 1 kip
Lebanon	100 piastres = 1 Lebanese pound
Lesotho	100 lisente = 1 (ma) Loti
Liberia	100 cents = 1 dollar
Libya	1000 dirhams = 1 dinar
Liechtenstein	100 rappen = 1 Swiss franc
Luxembourg	100 centimes = 1 Luxembourg franc
Macao	100 avos = 1 pataca
Madeira	100 centavos = 1 escudo
Malagasy Republic	5 francs = 1 ariary
Malawi	100 tambalas = 1 kwacha
Malaysia	100 cents = 1 Malaysian dollar
Maldive Islands	100 larees = 1 rupee
Mali	100 centimes = 1 CFA franc
Malta	100 cents = 1 Maltese pound
Marshall Islands	United States currency used
Mauritania	5 khoum = 1 ouguiya
Mauritius	100 cents = 1 rupee
Mexico	100 centavos = 1 peso
Micronesia	United States currency used
Monaco	100 centimes = 1 French franc

Mongolia	100 mung = 1 tugrik	St. Helena	100 pence = 1 pound sterling
Montserrat	100 cents = 1 East Caribbean dollar	St. Kitts	100 cents = 1 East Caribbean dollar
Morocco	100 francs = 1 dirham	St. Lucia	100 cents = 1 East Caribbean dollar
Mozambique	100 centavos = 1 meticul	St. Pierre and Miquelon	French currency used
		St. Thomas and Prince	
Namibia	100 cents = 1 rand	Islands	100 centavos = 1 dobra
Nauru	100 cents = 1 Australian dollar	St. Vincent	100 cents = 1 East Caribbean dollar
Nepal	100 paisa = 1 rupee	St. Vincent Grenadines	100 cents = 1 East Caribbean dollar
Netherlands	100 cents = 1 guilder	Samoa	100 sene = 1 tala
Netherlands Antilles	Netherlands currency used	San Marino	Italian currency used
Nevis	100 cents = 1 East Caribbean dollar	Saudi Arabia	100 halalahs = 1 riyal
New Caledonia	100 centimes = 1 CFP franc	Senegal	100 centimes = 1 CFA franc
New Zealand	100 cents = 1 New Zealand dollar	Seychelles	100 cents = 1 rupee
Nicaragua	100 centavos = 1 cordoba	Sierra Leone	100 cents = 1 leone
Niger	100 centimes = 1 CFA franc	Singapore	100 cents = 1 Singapore dollar
Nigeria	100 kobo = 1 naira	Solomon Islands	100 cents = 1 Australian dollar
Niuafo'ou	100 seniti = 1 pa'anga	Somalia	100 centesimi = 1 Somali shilling
Niue	100 cents = 1 New Zealand dollar	South Africa	100 cents = 1 rand
Norfolk Island	100 cents = 1 Australian dollar	South Georgia and South	
Norway	100 ore = 1 krone	Sandwich Islands	100 pence = 1 pound sterling
		Spain	100 centimos = 1 peseta
Oman	1000 baizas = 1 rial	Sri Lanka	100 cents = 1 Sri Lanka rupee
		Sudan	100 piastres = 1 Sudanese pound
Pakistan	100 paise = 1 rupee	Surinam	100 cents = 1 Surinam guilder
Palau	United States currency used	Swaziland	100 cents = 1 emalangeni
Panama	100 centesimos = 1 balboa	Sweden	100 ore = 1 krona
Papua New Guinea	100 toea = 1 kina	Switzerland	100 centimes = 1 Swiss franc
Paraguay	100 centimos = 1 guarani	Syria	100 piastres = 1 Syrian pound
Penrhyn Island	100 cents = 1 New Zealand dollar		
Peru	100 centimos = 1 inti	Tanzania	100 cents = 1 Tanzania shilling
Philippines	100 sentimos = 1 piso	Thailand	100 satangs = 1 baht
Pitcairn Islands	100 cents = 1 New Zealand dollar	Togo	100 centimes = 1 CFA franc
Poland	100 groszy = 1 zloty	Tokelau	100 cents = 1 New Zealand dollar
Portugal	100 centavos = 1 escudo	Tonga	100 senti = 1 pa'anga
		Transkei	100 cents = 1 South African rand
Qatar	100 dirhams = 1 rial	Trinidad and Tobago	100 cents = 1 Trinidad and Tobago dollar
		Tristan da Cunha	100 pence = 1 pound sterling
Rumania	100 bani = 1 leu	Tunisia	1000 milliemes = 1 dollar
Russia	100 kopecks = 1 rouble	Turkey	100 kurus = 1 lira
Rwanda	100 centimes = 1 Rwanda franc	Turks and Caicos Islands	100 cents = 1 U.S. dollar
		Tuvalu	100 cents = 1 Australian dollar

23

Uganda	100 cents = 1 Ugandan shilling
United Arab Emirates	100 fils = 1 dirham
United Nations	Austrian currency (Vienna issues);
	Swiss currency (Geneva issues);
	United States currency (New York issues)
United States of America	100 cents = 1 dollar
Uruguay	100 centesimos = 1 peso
Vanuatu	vatus
Vatican City	100 centesimi = 1 Italian lira
Venda	100 cents = 1 South African rand
Venezuela	100 centimos = 1 bolivar
Vietnam	100 xu = 1 dong
Wallis and Futuna Islands	100 centimes = 1 CFP franc
Yemen (Arab Republic)	100 fils = 1 riyal
Yemen (People's	
Democratic Republic)	1000 fils = 1 dinar
Yugoslavia	100 paras = 1 dinar
Zaire	100 makuta = 1 zaïre
Zambia	100 ngwee = 1 kwacha
Zil Elwannyen Sesel	100 cents = 1 rupee
Zimbabwe	100 cents = 1 Zimbabwe dollar